Pebble® Plus

Your Senses at the Grocery Store

by Kimberly M. Hutmacher

Consulting Editor: Gail Saunders-Smith, PhD

CAPSTONE PRESS
a capstone imprint

Pebble Plus is published by Capstone Press,
151 Good Counsel Drive, P.O. Box 669, Mankato, Minnesota 56002.
www.capstonepub.com

Books published by Capstone Press are manufactured with paper
containing at least 10 percent post-consumer waste.

Library of Congress Cataloging-in-Publication Data
Hutmacher, Kimberly.
  Your senses at the grocery store / by Kimberly M. Hutmacher.
    p. cm.—(Pebble plus. Out and about with your senses)
  Includes bibliographical references and index.
  Summary: "Simple text and full-color photographs describe using the five senses at the grocery store"—Provided by
publisher.
  ISBN 978-1-4296-6666-4 (library binding)
  1. Grocery shopping—Juvenile literature. 2. Supermarkets—Juvenile literature. 3. Senses and sensation—Juvenile
literature. I. Title.
  TX356H88 2012
  640.73—dc22   2010053940

Editorial Credits
Erika L. Shores, editor; Veronica Correia, designer; Svetlana Zhurkin, media researcher;
    Laura Manthe, production specialist

Photo Credits
All photos by Capstone Studio/Karon Dubke, except Shutterstock/Ilona Baha, cover (background)

Capstone thanks Kevin's Market in Lake Crystal, Minnesota, for their assistance with the photos in this book.

Note to Parents and Teachers

The Out and About with Your Senses series supports national standards related to life science.
This book describes and illustrates using the five senses at the grocery store. The images support
early readers in understanding the text. The repetition of words and phrases helps early readers
learn new words. This book also introduces early readers to subject-specific vocabulary words,
which are defined in the Glossary section. Early readers may need assistance to read some words
and to use the Table of Contents, Glossary, Read More, Internet Sites, and Index sections of
the book.

Printed in the United States of America in North Mankato, Minnesota.
032011
006110CGF11

Table of Contents

Off to the Store!

Watch the big glass doors slide open. Feel the cart's smooth handle. Let's use our five senses at the grocery store.

What We See

Look! Produce shelves burst
with colorful fruit.
Bright bunches of
yellow bananas sit in rows.

Count the orange, white,

and yellow cheeses

in the dairy aisle.

What We Hear

What do you hear?

Wheels on carts squeak.

Friends chat.

Snappy music plays.

What We Touch

Feel the rough pineapple.

Customers squeeze fruits

to see if they are ripe.

Brrr. We might need a jacket

in the frozen food aisle.

Ice cream feels cold.

A bag of frozen broccoli

feels bumpy.

What We Smell

Sniff, sniff.

The scent of laundry soap

and bleach fills the air.

Fabric sheets smell like flowers.

What We Taste

Sample stands dot the aisles.

We get to taste some food

they're selling.

Try some spicy cheese.

Look at our full cart!

We've used all five senses

on our trip to the store.

It's time to go home

and taste some yummy food.

Glossary

aisle—a walkway between shelves

dairy—having to do with milk products

fabric—cloth or a soft material

produce—fruits and vegetables

ripe—ready to eat

sample—a small amount of something to try

sense—a way of knowing about your surroundings; hearing, smelling, touching, tasting, and seeing are the five senses

Read More

Chancellor, Deborah. *I Wonder Why Lemons Taste Sour and Other Questions about the Senses.* Boston: Kingfisher, 2007.

Feldman, Jean, and Holly Karapetkova. *Five Senses.* Vero Beach, Fla.: Rourke Pub., 2010.

Kalman, Bobbie. *My Senses Help Me.* My World. New York: Crabtree Pub., 2010.

Internet Sites

FactHound offers a safe, fun way to find Internet sites related to this book. All of the sites on FactHound have been researched by our staff.

Here's all you do:

Visit *www.facthound.com*

Type in this code: 9781429666664

Index

Word Count: 155
Grade: 1
Early-Intervention Level: 15